Dalek, alias James Marshall, est l'un des artistes les pl
tique de Brooklyn. Titulaire du BFA de l'Institut d'art de ᵕ   ᵕ art urbain,
de la culture graffiti et télévisuelle. Ses travaux ont été exposés à Londres, à New York ainsi qu'au
musée d'Art contemporain de Washington ou encore à la Galerie Magda Danysz à Paris.
Son style est en cohérence avec sa profonde conviction qu'il existe un monde meilleur : son
pinceau dessine les contours de personnages colorés, pleins de vie et d'humour.
Dalek parle très peu de son travail, mais un jour il m'a déclaré : « Le monde serait mieux s'il était
tout en rose ». Un tel précepte montre qu'il y a tant à comprendre chez cet artiste qui nous offre
une vision intransigeante du monde tel qu'il est mais aussi l'espoir d'un monde meilleur. Dès notre
première rencontre, j'ai compris que son travail était constitué de ces contradictions. Celles que
nous portons tous en nous, au quotidien.
Comment décrire l'artiste lui-même ? James est une montagne de gentillesse. Cet homme

James Marshall, a.k.a. Dalek, is one of the most original artists to emerge from Brooklyn's artistic
scene. A fine arts graduate from the Art Institute of Chicago, he primarily draws his inspiration
from urban art and from graffiti and TV culture. His work has been shown in London, New York,
at the Museum of Contemporary Art in Washington and at the Galerie Magda Danysz in Paris.
His style is in tune with his deep conviction that a better world is possible: his brush creates
colourful characters brimming with life and humour.
Dalek talks very little about his work, but he once told me "the world would look much better if it
were bright pink". With such a precept, there is much to understand about this artist, who offers
us an intransigent vision of the world as it is but also the hope he cherishes for a better one. The
very first time we met, I understood that his work grows out of these contradictions – those that
each of us carries inside, from day to day.

impressionnant par sa taille l'est aussi par son regard sur le monde. Droit et sans concessions. Il s'exprime par la peinture plus que par les mots et réussit à se faire entendre *à première vue*.

J'ai toujours en mémoire ce premier rendez-vous où j'ai vu arriver James. Nous devions nous rencontrer, comme une évidence, pour faire équipe. Je voulais tant porter sa vision du monde au public. De cet entretien me reste en mémoire surtout sa détermination. Ses paroles sont aussi nettes que son trait. Tout chez lui est précision.

À la question « qui es-tu ? », Dalek ne répond que très rarement. Il déteste cette question. Il est lui-même. Avec le temps, seulement, on apprend à le connaître, lui et son univers artistique.

Pour la petite histoire, Dalek a commencé à construire son monde dès l'enfance. Un monde très inspiré de l'univers télévisuel et de dessins dans lesquels il se réfugie à l'époque. Il commence à peindre sur les murs vers l'âge de 25 ans. Un ami lui demande, quelques années plus tard, une œuvre représentant son personnage, et c'est alors que Dalek passe à la peinture sur toile. Chacune

How to describe the artist himself? James is a mountain of kindness. He compels attention because of his height but also his outlook on the world. Upright and uncompromising. He expresses himself more by painting than by words, and manages to make himself heard at first sight.

I can still remember our first encounter. I saw James arrive, and it seemed obvious to me that we were supposed to meet and team up. I so wanted to bring his vision of the world to the public. What I most remember about our talk was his determination. His words were as clear-cut as his linestyle. Everything about him is precise.

When asked "who are you?", Dalek rarely replies. He hates that question. He's him. Only over time do you get to know him and his artistic universe.

A footnote: Dalek was a child when he began building his world. A world greatly inspired by the television programmes and drawings in which he took refuge at the time. He began painting walls

de ses rencontres avec l'art a été plus instinctive, profonde, que construite. Il a peint, évolué, appris, seul principalement, et développé son univers.

Ses brefs passages à l'Art Institute de Chicago et, plus tard, à l'Université de Virginia-Commonwealth lui ont permis d'étudier respectivement la photographie et la peinture. Mais il ne termine pas ce cursus. Tout cela lui paraît trop lent. Il préfère partir pour New York.

Le style qu'il a ainsi développé au fil du temps est difficile à décrire. Il le qualifie lui-même, peut-être en hommage – plus ou moins consciemment – à Freud, d'«analement absurde».

Mais au fond, pour connaître Dalek, ne faut-il pas apprivoiser ses Space Monkeys ? Sans pouvoir répondre de façon complète à la question récurrente : qui sont les Space Monkeys ?, j'ai avec le temps réussi à les observer. Par leurs formes, ils me font penser à ces figures peintes par Picasso. Jamais un profil ne correspond vraiment à la réalité, il s'agit plus de perception. Une vision tordue du monde, des visages, cependant cachés à dessein par leur profil, à l'image de tout ce que l'hu-

around the age of 25. A few years later, a friend asked him to paint his character for him, which was how Dalek switched to canvas. Each of his encounters with art has been more instinctive and profound than engineered. He has painted, evolved, learnt, mainly by himself, and developed his universe.

At the Art Institute of Chicago, and later at the Virginia Commonwealth University, he studied photography and painting respectively. But he didn't complete the latter course. It seemed to be dragging its feet. He preferred to move to New York.

The style he has developed over time is hard to describe. He himself terms it – perhaps in a more or less conscious tribute to Freud – as "anally absurd".

But to get to the bottom of Dalek you probably need to tame his Space Monkeys. Though unable to fully answer the recurrent question of who the Space Monkeys are, I have over time been able

main dissimule si souvent. Parfois perçus comme formellement trop simplistes par leurs détracteurs, les Space Monkeys sont les personnages récurrents des œuvres de Dalek et deviennent une métaphore de l'homme. Ils ne révèlent leur richesse intérieure qu'à ceux qui veulent bien dialoguer avec eux.

À travers sa peinture, à la manière des plus grands photographes, Dalek distille des émotions, des engagements et des idées fortes. Comme le faisait le photographe Richard Avedon dans ses portraits, Dalek nous offre des sourires grinçants pleins de sous-entendus, des yeux emplis d'éloquence et des crânes dégarnis marqués par la vie. Ne retrouve-t-on pas dans ces Space Monkeys un peu du front de Jorge Louis Borges, du sourire de Vladimir Horowitz, des yeux de Jean Renoir ou de la mâchoire de Jean Cocteau ?

Dalek se joue de l'homme à travers les Space Monkeys. Leurs têtes apparaissent souvent trouées, comme évidées – métaphore de l'homme et de son manque de cervelle –, souvent ils se cognent

to observe them. Their shapes make me think of those figures Picasso painted. The profiles never really fit reality, it's more a perception. A twisted vision of the world, of heads, whose profile, however, intentionally masks the face, like everything that humans so often conceal.

The Space Monkeys, whose detractors sometimes find their forms simplistic, are recurring characters in Dalek's work and become a metaphor for humankind. They reveal their rich interior life only to those willing to converse with them.

Through his painting, Dalek, as with the greatest photographers, distils emotions, commitments and very strong ideas. Like the photographer Richard Avedon in his portraits, Dalek offers us creaking smiles heavy with subtext, eyes full of eloquence, and bald skulls marked by life. Don't these Space Monkeys have something of the forehead of Jorge Luis Borges, the smile of Vladimir Horowitz, the eyes of Jean Renoir and the jawline of Jean Cocteau?

la tête – l'homme, par nature, se rend fou lui-même – et parfois ils pètent car, aux dires de l'artiste, « les hommes feraient mieux de péter que de parler ». Lewis Carroll aurait pu répondre à cela, tel le cavalier qui croise Alice : « La position dans laquelle se trouve mon corps n'a aucune espèce d'importance. Mon esprit fonctionne tout aussi bien. En fait, plus j'ai la tête en bas, plus j'invente de choses nouvelles. »

Reflet de la nature humaine, les Space Monkeys cumulent nos tares, mais restent attachants. Ils sont partout. On les retrouve sur les boîtes de Krylon en hommage à la période graffiti de l'artiste. Sur les pochettes de disque qui constituent notre culture musicale. Ils sont tour à tour dangereux, armés de haches et de couteaux, ou guerriers couards tapis sous des canons de chars blindés, souffrant de leurs membres amputés.

Ils avancent et semblent aussi se marrer franchement ; se rire de la vie ; être dirigés par des forces politiques supérieures ou encore obéir à des forces occultes. À moins qu'ils ne soient juste tombés

Dalek pokes fun at humankind through the Space Monkeys. Their heads often seem to have holes, as if emptied out – a metaphor for Man and his brainlessness; and they are often banging their heads – it is Man's nature to send himself mad – and sometimes they fart, because, says the artist, "people would be better farting than talking". Lewis Carroll might have replied, like the horseman who comes across Alice, that "the position of my body is of no importance. My mind works just as well. In fact, the lower my head is, the more things I invent".

A reflection of human nature, the Space Monkeys are an anthology of our flaws but engaging all the same. They are everywhere. On Krylon boxes in homage to the artist's graffiti period. On the disc covers that make up our musical culture. Sometimes they are dangerous individuals armed with axes and knives, or lily-livered warriors cowering under tank cannons, distressed by their blown-off limbs.

sur la tête. Le Petit Prince de Saint-Exupéry affirme d'ailleurs : « Les hommes s'enfournent dans les rapides, mais ils ne savent plus ce qu'ils cherchent. Alors ils s'agitent et tournent en rond... » Les Space Monkeys n'en sont pas moins observateurs. Avec leur œil, certes unique mais dispro-portionné, ils voient tout.

Dalek nous offre aussi sa vision du monde à travers son travail photographique. Un travail net. Ses images permettent d'entrevoir les couleurs du monde, de notre environnement, du voisinage. Ces touches de lumière à l'image de l'espoir que l'artiste nourrit envers l'humanité.

Ainsi, Dalek s'inspire du monde et peint sans fin ses absurdités. L'incohérence de l'humanité est à ses yeux un feuilleton télévisé permanent : « une sitcom 24 heures sur 24 », comme il aime à le souligner. Les Space Monkeys c'est vous, c'est moi, tout un chacun. Peut-être un peu plus lui que nous, et encore...

En matière de style, Dalek est cohérent et constant dans sa forme. Sa technique est impression-

They keep moving forward and also seem to be having a right old giggle; laughing at life; being led by higher political forces, or in thrall to occult powers. Unless, that is, they've just banged their heads. Indeed Saint Exupéry's Little Prince noted: "Men rush down the rapids, but they no longer know what they are looking for. So they get all worked up and go round in circles...".

The Space Monkeys are observers, nonetheless. With their eye, unique yet disproportionate, they see everything. But Dalek also offers us his vision of the world through his photography. The work is clear-cut. In his images we glimpse the colours of our world, our surroundings, our neighbour-hood. Touches of light like the hopes the artist nurtures for humanity.

Dalek taps the world for inspiration and endlessly paints its absurdities. The incoherence of humanity is, as he enjoys pointing out, "a 24-hour sitcom". The Space Monkeys are you, me, everyone. Though maybe him a bit more than us, and then some...

nante, une peinture lisse et proche de la perfection, qu'il a appliquée lorsqu'il travaillait pour Takashi Murakami.

Aujourd'hui, il collabore, le temps d'une exposition, avec un autre artiste américain : Shepard Fairey. Chacun d'eux, riche de son propre style, fait écho à l'autre.

Quand Dalek est plutôt inspiré par la bande dessinée et le graffiti, Shepard Fairey, également connu sous le nom de Obey Giant, réalise des stickers et des affiches qu'il colle sur les murs des villes. Les codes visuels utilisés par Shepard Fairey sont dignes de ceux de la propagande stalinienne. En collant ses affiches dans le monde entier, son but n'est pas seulement de provoquer, mais surtout de mettre en évidence les mécanismes de propagande publicitaire qui envahissent l'espace public. Ainsi, son travail tendrait à « permettre aux gens de voir clairement ce qui est devant leurs yeux mais qui leur reste caché ».

Derrière des œuvres graphiquement très différentes, tant par les supports utilisés que par les traits

In terms of style, Dalek is coherent and constant in form. He has an impressive technique, a smooth, near-perfect way with paint, which he used when working for Takashi Murakami.

He now collaborates, on occasional exhibitions, with another American artist, Shepard Fairey. Their rich styles echo one another.

Whereas Dalek is mainly inspired by comics and graffiti, Shepard Fairey, a.k.a. Obey Giant, makes stickers and posters which he puts up on city walls. Fairey's visual codes are worthy of Stalinist propaganda. In displaying his posters all over the world, he aims to provoke but primarily to highlight the advertising-propaganda mechanisms that are invading the public space. His work tends to "enable people to clearly see what's in front of their eyes but remains hidden from them".

Behind two bodies of work that are graphically very different, in their media and their linestyles and colours, there is a unity of meaning. Dalek and Fairey denounce dictatorship in all its forms,

et les couleurs, se cache une unité de sens. Dalek et Shepard Fairey dénoncent la dictature sous toutes ses formes, qu'elle soit politique, économique ou intellectuelle. Un message aussi fort que celui que voulait porter le peintre Diego Rivera en d'autres temps, mais exprimé plus à la manière du créateur des Simpsons, Matt Groening.

Magda Danysz

Galeriste

be it political, economic or intellectual. It is a message as strong as the one that painter Diego Rivera wished to convey in a different era, but which is expressed here more in the manner of the Simpsons' creator, Matt Groening.

Magda Danysz

Gallery owner

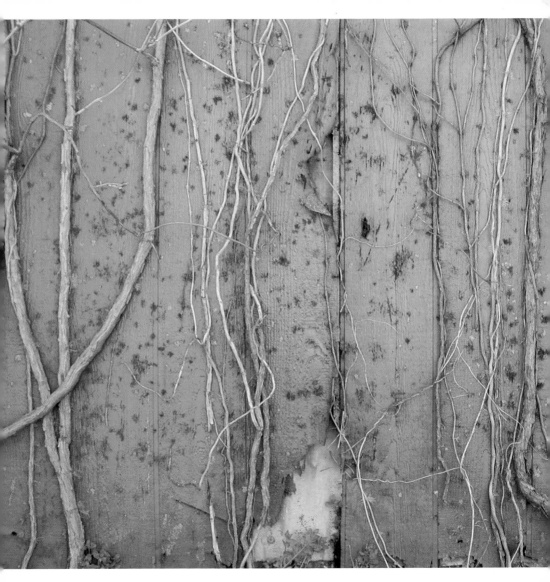

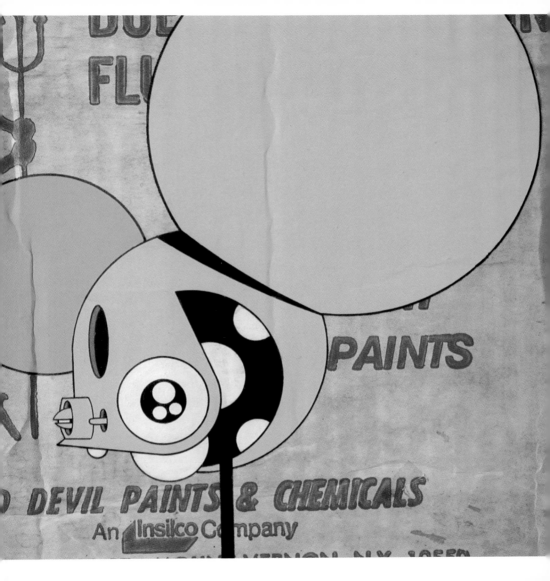

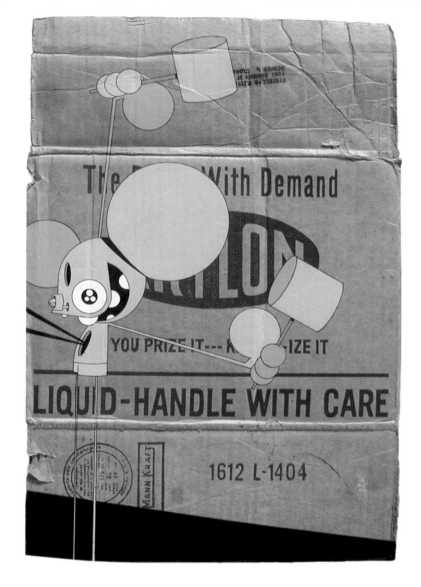

SOUTH PACIFIC
Orchestra Conducted by AL GOODMAN

Side A	Side B
OVERTURE	ENTRE - ACTE
SOME ENCHANTED EVENING	YOUNGER THAN SPRINGTIME
THERE'S NOTHING LIKE A DAME	I'M GONNA WASH THAT MAN
BALI HA'I	RIGHT OUT OF MY HAIR
WONDERFUL GUY	THIS NEARLY WAS MINE
	HAPPY TALK
	FINALE

RICHARD TORIGI

Richard Torigi, featured vocalist on this album was born Santo Tortorigi in the Bay Ridge section of Brooklyn, N. Y.

Mr. Torigi has been singing professionally since he was 16 years old. World War II, however, interrupted his career for four years. He saw combat as a radar flying officer in the South Pacific.

Returning home, he joined the New York Opera Company in 1950, singing with them for five years. He also performed with distinction as a member of the Wagner and San Carlo Opera Companies.

Many of the leading opera troupes, groups and repertories have featured him. He has appeared with various companies in New Orleans, Chicago, San Francisco, Pittsburgh and Cincinnati. His most recent Broadway appearance was the lead in "The Most Happy Fella". When not employed in singing roles, Mr. Torigi finds a creative outlet in his sculpturing.

SOUTH PACIFIC

South Pacific had a phenomenal run at the Majestic Theatre in New York City. It has been revived by various theatre groups throughout the country — bidding fair to become a veritable staple of show business. The latest production of South Pacific is the current lavishly produced screen-version.

The story of the show deals with ⸻ of sailors and marines on a tropical ⸻ War II. Nellie, the heroine of the ⸻ Rock, U. S. A.

Nellie meets and falls in love with ⸻ French planter, Emile, already the prou⸻ by a Polynesian wife.

Inevitably the lovers break up, with ⸻ man right out of my hair" and Emi⸻ agent for our side — spying on ene⸻ When Emile returns to his plantation, h⸻ for him — and the curtain falls on an ⸻

An opening night critic on the me⸻ South Pacific in 1949 said, in commen⸻ "The Rodgers music is his finest—fitting ⸻ of South Pacific so well. It is filled with Ha⸻ he said⸻

⸻ere Is Nothing Like A Dame, Some ⸻ A ⸻ful Guy, Younger Than Springt⸻ ⸻ Happy Talk" I'm Gonn⸻ ⸻ Hair, have become so⸻ ⸻bout.

AL GOODMAN

AL GOODMAN famous conductor and musician has devoted all his life to music. His love for music and his inherent musical ability were manifest at an early age when he sang soprano in his father's choir, became a musician in the pit of a local "movie house", and was awarded a scholarship to the Peabody Conservatory in Baltimore.

In 1915 Al Goodman was selected by Earl Carroll to accompany him to California as arranger and conductor. That was Goodman's official entry into show business . . . that start of an illustrious musical career which brought him into personal contact with the all-time "greats" of show business . . . as the conductor of many shows and musical production whose successes were due in great measure to his outstanding ability.

Al Goodman produced musical comedies with Earl Carroll . . . never-to-be forgotten hits like "So Long Letty" and "Canary Cottage". He became Al Jolson's personal conductor and arranger, then J. J. Shubert made him general musical director and composer of all Shubert musical productions. He later became associated with various Radio and TV Shows as musical consultant and director such as the Hit Parade & the Colgate Hour. In his wide and varied career he was associated arranger, conductor, recording artist or musical supervisor for about 200 famous musical shows and programs. He has worked with the biggest names in the history of Broadway: Earl Carroll, Al Jolson, George White, Sigmund Romberg, Jack Benny, Fannie Brice, George Jessel, Flo Ziegfeld, James Melton, Max Gordon, Bob Hope, and many, many others.

The name of Al Goodman, arranger, conductor, musician is one of the brightest lights of show business on Broadway.

Whenever you buy a Diplomat Album you are buying one ⸻ the greatest record values in the world. The quality of the material used in its manufacture; the exclusive process employed in the pressings; the fine protective nature of its packag⸻ ⸻erior method of HI-FI recording technique and the ⸻ ⸻ ing, all contribute their part in producing a⸻ album, is of equal quality to brands costing ⸻ more. We urge you to handle this record ca⸻ best needles and treat it kindly. If you d⸻ ⸻

This recording you have ⸻hased was made on an ⸻ ⸻ Recorder, Model 360 ⸻ Altec ⸻Telefunken Micro⸻ The Master ⸻ing cut on a ⸻ Lathe with Gra⸻ton Fe⸻ Cutter Heads driven b⸻ designed 200 Watt Amplifi⸻ Mastering was done with ⸻ mum stylus velocity cons⸻ with minimum distortion ⸻

⸻NICAL DATA (R⸻

Although the total frequency ran⸻ of 16 CPS to 25,000 CPS on ⸻ record is not with the ra⸻ of ordinary ⸻ examination ⸻ ⸻ ings of the ⸻ quencies. How⸻ ⸻ion of the po⸻ that the r⸻ ⸻le ⸻

16 CPS		
		25,000 CPS

⸻ DIPLOMAT RECORDS ⸻

This is a Diplomat Long Playing 33⅓ RPM Record, unbreakable under normal use. For greater enjoyment ⸻ should always be kept away fr⸻ Dust and dirt should be removed from this record wit⸻ lint free cloth.

⸻ted in U.S.A.

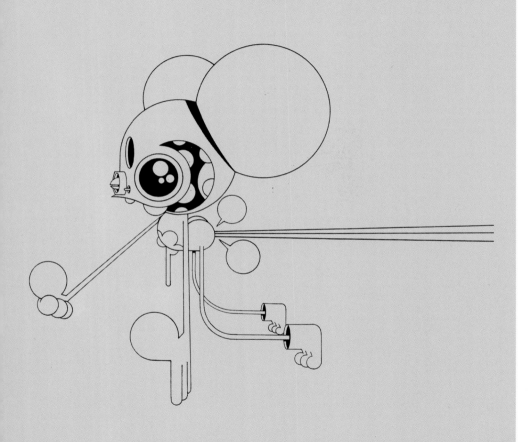

PROJECT: PARKVIEW ESTATES 20 BAYARD ST.
OWNER: 20 BAYARD ST. WILLIAMSBURG, NY 11211

TO ANONYMOUSLY REPORT UNSAFE
CONDITIONS AT THIS WORK SITE CALL 311

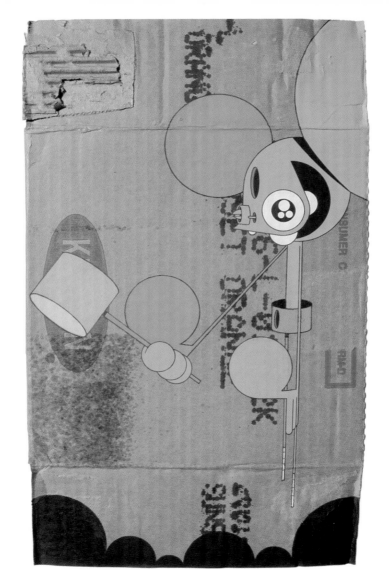

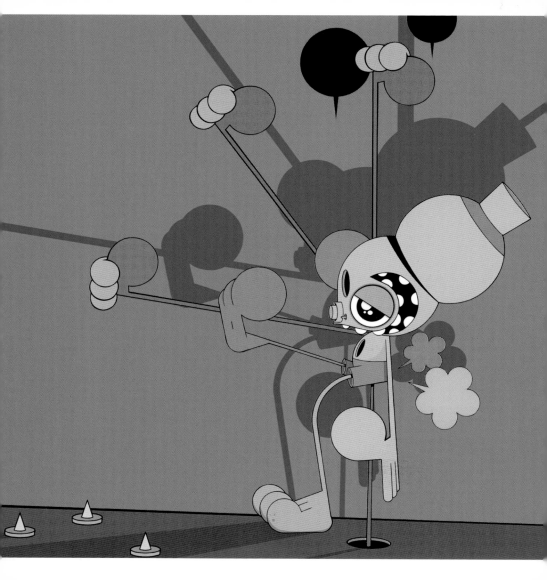

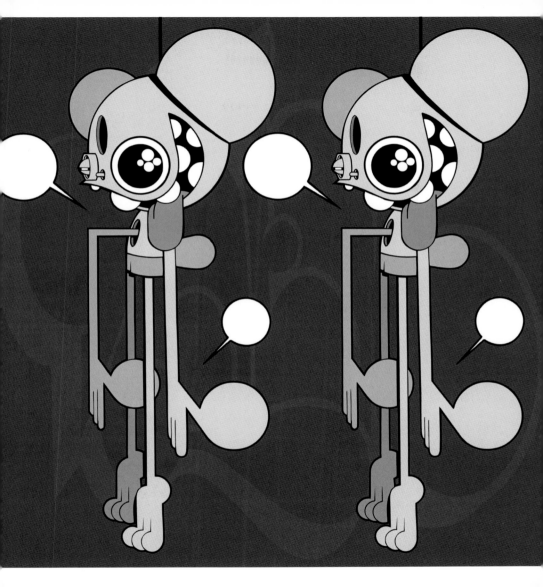

DE'S AUTO REPAIR CORNER

CAR & TRUCK SUNDAY

UP TO 18,000LBS

PECTIONS

CIAL INSPECTION STATION #7056614

O **REPAIR**

FOREIGN & DOMESTIC 782-

Phone

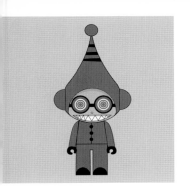

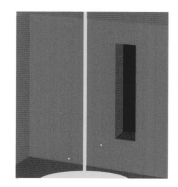

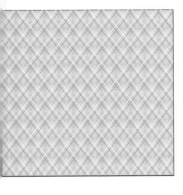

Sweet Revenge

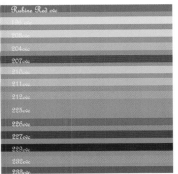

Rubine Red c+c

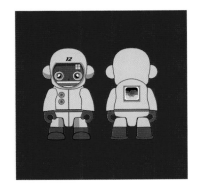

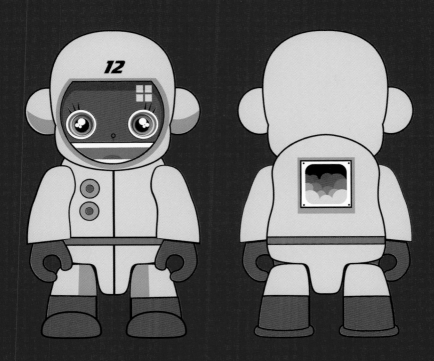

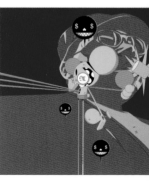

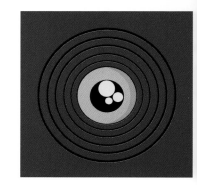

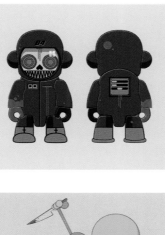

Sweet Apathy

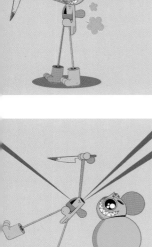

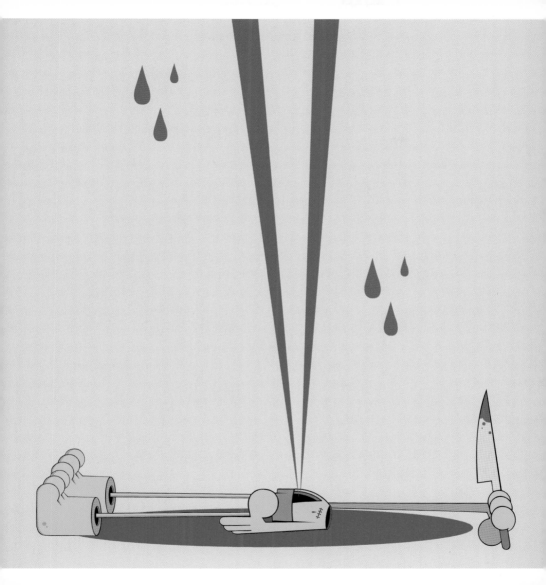

..the criminal was described as Hispanic

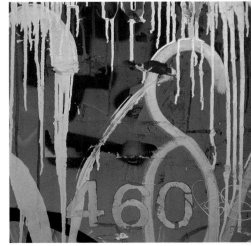

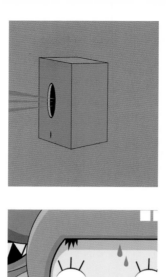
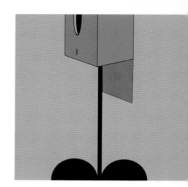

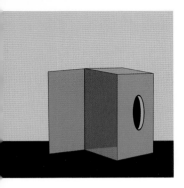

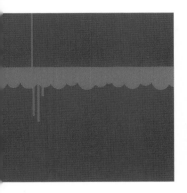

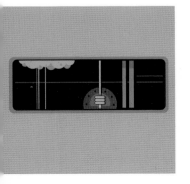

THE GODS
ARE POUNDING
MY HEAD!
(AKA LUMBERJACK MESSIAH)

Written and directed by
RICHARD
FOREMAN

ological Theater at St Mark's Church 2nd Ave & 10th Street
www.ontological.com Tel: 212 533-4650

THE GODS
ARE POUNDING
MY HEAD!
(AKA LUMBERJACK MESSIAH)

Written and directed by
RICHARD
FOREMAN

Ontological Theater at St Mark's Church 2nd Ave & 10th Str
www.ontological.com Tel: 212 533-46

THE GODS
ARE POUNDING
MY HEAD!
(AKA LUMBERJACK MESSIAH)

Written and directed by
RICHARD
FOREMAN

Ontological Theater at St Mark's Church 2nd Ave & 10th Street
www.ontological.com Tel: 212 533-4650

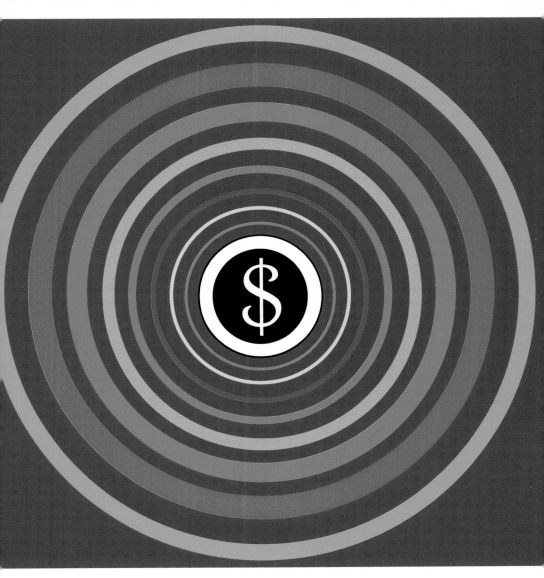

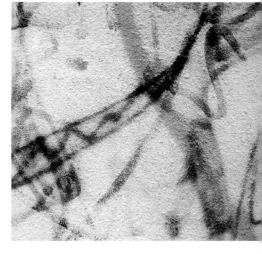

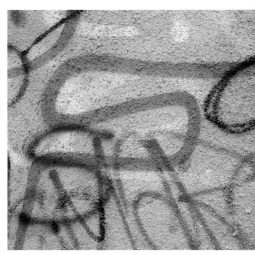

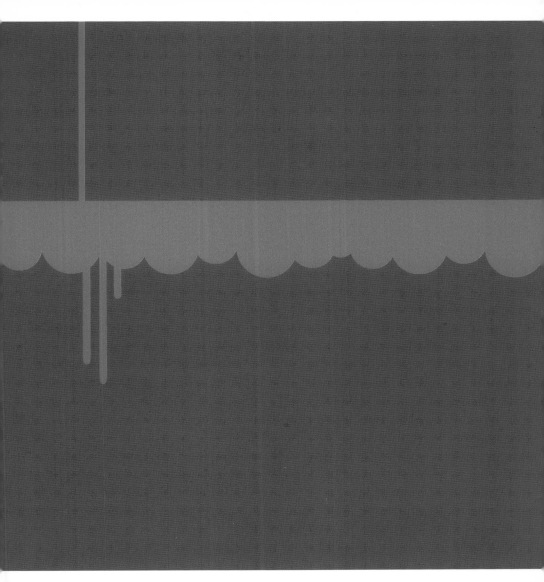

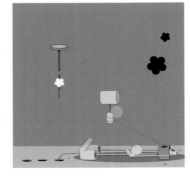

WARNING
KEEP OUT
POISON | BAITED AREA |

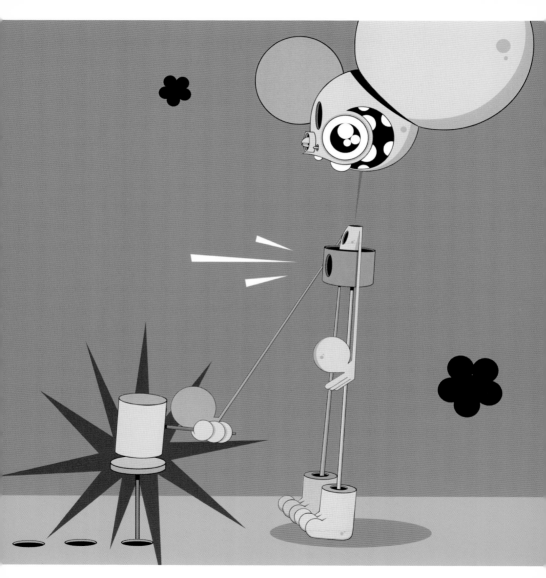

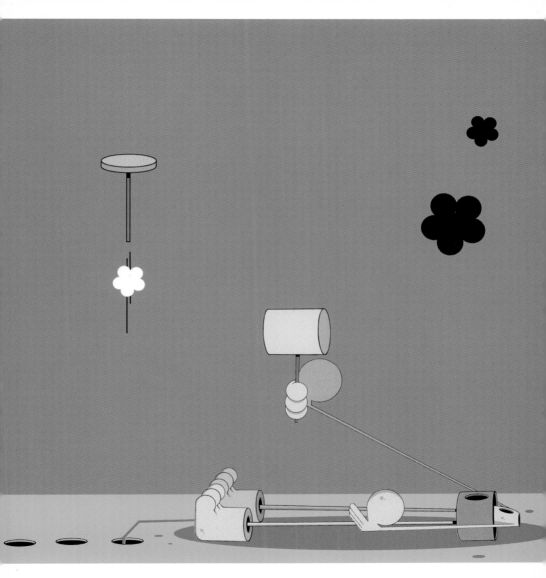

LÉGENDES / CAPTIONS

Tous les travaux présentés dans cet ouvrage datent de 2005. La plupart des photos ont été prises à Brooklyn. / All the featured work is from 2005. Most of the photos were taken in Brooklyn.

BIOGRAPHIE / BIOGRAPHY

Born

New London, Connecticut / May 22 1968

Education

B.S. from Virginia Commonwealth University / 1992

B.F.A. from the School of the Art Institute of Chicago / 1995

EXPOSITION / EXHIBITIONS

111 Minna St. Gallery, San Francisco CA. Feb. 2000 / Dec. 2003 (group) • New Image Art: Los Angeles, CA. March 2001 (group) • 381 G Gallery: San Francisco, CA. Jan. 2001 (solo) • WDWA: Brooklyn NY. Sept. 2001 (solo) • MOCA DC: Washington DC. Oct. 2001 / March 2003 (group) • Upper Playground: San Francisco, CA. Dec. 2001 (group) / Dec. 2004 (group) • Max Fish: NYC. Feb. 2002 (group) • Merry Karnowsky Gallery: Los Angeles, CA. Feb. 2002 (group) • The Front Room: Brooklyn NY. April 2002 (group) • Luxe Projects: NYC. April 2002 (group) • Alife: NYC. April 2002 / Dec. 2003 (group) • Eighth Floor Artist Corp.: NYC. June 2002 / Aug. 2003 (group) • New Image Art: Los Angeles, CA. June 2002 (group) • Apart Gallery: London, England. July 2002 (group) • Rocket Gallery: Tokyo, Japan. Sept. 2002 / July 2003 (group) • Pamela Auchincloss / Project Space: NYC. Oct. 2002 (group) • Black Market: Los Angeles CA. Nov. 2002 (group) • Deitch Projects: NYC. Dec. 2002 (group) • Parco Gallery: Nagoya. Japan. Feb. 2003 (group) • OX-OP Gallery: Minneapolis MN. April 2003 (solo) / Dec. 2004 (solo) • McCaig-Welles Gallery: Brooklyn NY. April 2003 (group) • Compound Gallery: Portland OR. June 2003 (solo) • Washington St. Art Center: Somerville, MA. June 2003 (group) • Contemporary Art Center of Virginia: Virginia Beach. July 2003 (group) • Heaven Gallery: Chicago IL. July 2003 (group) • Merry Karnowsky Gallery: Los Angeles. August 2003 (solo) • Lump

Gallery: Raleigh NC. Sept. 2003 (solo) • Colette: Paris. Oct. 2003 (group) • Asian American Arts Centre: NYC. Nov. 2003 (group) • Paul Rodgers 9w gallery: NYC. Jan. 2004 (group) • Cincinnati Art Center: Cincinnati, OH. March 2004 (group) • Magda Danysz: Paris. May 2004 (solo) • Yerba Buena Center for the Arts: San Francisco. July 2004 (group) • Merry Karnowsky Gallery: Los Angeles: Aug. 2004 (solo) • Best: London. Sept. 2004 (solo) • McCaig-Welles Gallery: Brooklyn NY. Jan. 2005 (solo) • Jonathan LeVine Gallery: NYC. Feb. 2005 (group) • Art Prostitute Gallery: Dallas TX. Feb. 2005 (group) • Clemintine Gallery: NYC. March 2005 (group)

Upcoming : Magda Danysz: Paris, June 2005, 2 Man Show with Shepard Fairey • 222 Gallery: Philadelphia, PA, June 2005 (solo) • Le Gallery: Toronto, ON, July 2005 (solo) • Merry Karnowsky Gallery: Los Angeles, August 2005 (solo) • Jonathan LeVine Gallery: NYC, Oct. 2005 (solo)

PUBLICATIONS

Art Week: Jan. 2000 • Art Papers: Jan. / Feb 2001 • San Francisco Guardian: Feb. 2001 • Arkitip: July 2001 • Flux Magazine: July 2001 • The Kansas City Star: July 2001 • Mass Appeal: Dec. 2001 • Juxtapoz: March / April 2002 ; Sept. / Oct. 2002 • Tokion: March / April 2002 ; June / July 2002 • NYARTS: June 2002 • While You Were Sleeping: June 2000 ; July 2002 • Colorado Daily: July 2002 • Pour La Victoire: published by Surface to Air: Aug. 2002 • Philadelphia City Paper: Aug. 2002 • Relax: Nov. 2002 • New American Paintings: Issue 44. Feb. 2003 • Eye: Issue 47. Spring 2003 • D Art International : March 2003 • Pioneer Press (St.Paul Mn.) April 2003 • Dalek: Nickel plated angels, Gingko Press: April 2003 • Washington Post: May 2003 • New York Resident: June 2003 • Strength Magazine: June 2003 • The Sponsorship Book: published by Ryan McGiness, Sept. 2003 • Pictoplasma 2: published by Die Gestalten Verlag, Oct. 2003 • Morning Wood: published by Gingko Press, Nov. 2003 • Heavy: published by alife / neverstop, Dec. 2003 • New York Times: Dec. 26th 2003 • Juxtapoz: Summer Special Issue, Summer 2004 • The Wall St. Journal: Nov. 12th 2004 • New York Magazine: Nov. 29th 2004 • Refill Magazine: Issue #4, Winter 2004 • City Magazine: Feb. / March 2005 • Elemental Magazine: March 2005 • Trace: March 2005 • Washington Post: March 27th 2005 • Paper Magazine: April 2005 • V Magazine: April 2005 • Dalek: Sonic Order of Hapiness, R77 Press, April 2005

AUTRES INFORMATIONS / OTHER INFORMATIONS

Assistant to Takashi Murakami: Oct. 2001 / March 2002
Instructor: Virginia Commonwealth University: Jan. 2001 / May 2001
City of Baltimore Artscape 2002 (public art project): July 2002 / July 2003
Visiting artist / Guest lecturer: Kansas City Art Institute, March 2003
Paintura Projects / Graffiti meets Windows 2003: Osaka, Japan, July 2003
Rock the vote / Spiewak benefit: NYC, Oct. 2004
AIGA: silent auction to benefit AIGA Mentoring program
Scope Art Fair NY / Galerie Magda Danysz: March 2005

www.dalekart.com
Dalek est représenté en France par la galerie Magda Danysz : www.magda-gallery.com